CARING FOR
MY NEW
PARAKEET

John Bankston

HOW TO CARE FOR YOUR NEW PET

Mitchell Lane

PUBLISHERS

2001 SW 31st Avenue
Hallandale, FL 33009
www.mitchelllane.com

First Edition, 2021.

Author: John Bankston
Designer: Ed Morgan
Editor: Morgan Brody

Names/credits:
Title: Caring for My New Parakeet / by John Bankston
Description: Hallandale, FL : Mitchell Lane Publishers

Series: How to Care for Your New Pet

Library bound ISBN: 978-1-58415-166-1

eBook ISBN: 978-1-58415-169-2

Photo credits: Freepik.com, Shutterstock

CONTENTS

Words in **bold** throughout can
be found in the Glossary.

Popular Parakeets

With their cheerful chatter and colorful feathers, parakeets make wonderful pets. Parakeets are sweet, **social** little birds that enjoy interaction with each other and with their human **companions**. Some can even be taught to talk.

Parakeets surprise their owners. They cuddle like dogs. They learn words just like toddlers. Parrots and parakeets don't **mimic**. They understand words' meaning.

Parakeets are not for everyone. They need a lot of care. They can be demanding. Some don't speak. But if you want a bird, parakeets are a great choice. Just make sure you learn their **habits**. That's the best way to keep them happy. Although they are relatively easy to care for, they do have special requirements.

DID YOU KNOW?
Parakeets are also called "Budgerigar" (buhj-uh-ree-gahr).

Parakeet Facts

Parakeets are a favorite pet. Most are friendly and very gentle. The birds are also called "budgies." They are part of the parrot family. Parakeets are the world's second smallest type of parrot.

Parakeets became **popular** pets in the 1800s. John Gould brought them to Europe from Australia. In 1894, Australia made this against the law. Europeans began **breeding** pet parakeets. In the U.S., the birds became popular in the 1950s.

Parakeets are easy to train. They are social birds. Many people have two parakeets. If you only get one, you'll need to spend more time with it. Parakeets **bond** with the person who takes care of them.

These playful pets are seven to ten inches long. Wild parakeets are mostly green and yellow. You can find budgies in almost every color of the rainbow, except red and pink. They are so colorful; they sometimes remind people of jellybeans!

DID YOU KNOW?
The word parakeet literally means "long tail."

Parakeet Prep

Life changes with a new pet. You might have to walk your dog in the rain. Playing hamsters can wake you up. Pet parakeets spend a lot of time in their cage. Yet they will still change your life.

Lots of things that are fine for dogs and cats make birds sick. Nonstick pans release **fumes** when they are heated. These fumes can hurt parakeets. Oven cleaners are also bad. No one should use these things when your bird is home— even if it is kept far from the kitchen. Fumes travel.

Smoke and air fresheners can also make your bird sick.

Your parakeet's cage gives it a safe place to eat and sleep. The best cage is the biggest one you can buy. Small birds love big cages. Make sure the bars are less than half an inch apart. This keeps your parakeet from escaping or getting stuck. The cage should not have sharp edges. It should be at least two feet long and two feet wide. The longer the cage, the better. It should also be at least two feet tall.

DID YOU KNOW?

In the U.S., nearly six million homes have over 16 million pet birds.

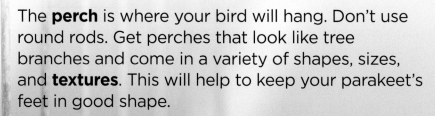

The **perch** is where your bird will hang. Don't use round rods. Get perches that look like tree branches and come in a variety of shapes, sizes, and **textures**. This will help to keep your parakeet's feet in good shape.

Food and water bowls should not be under the perches. Put them in the corner of the cage. You can also use hanging cups. Parakeets like to be clean, so you may add a bathing pool. Water needs to be changed at least once a day. Bowls should be cleaned daily. Line the cage with newspaper.

Bedding made of pellets, corn cob, or wood shavings are very bad for parakeets.

Change the paper every day. Make a mix two-thirds water and one-third vinegar. Put this in a spray bottle. Use this to clean the cage every week.

Parakeets do best when they are around people. Your parakeet might like being in the living room or TV room. Don't put the cage near a window. Do not put it in the kitchen. The cage should not be on the floor. The back should be against a wall. Don't put it right in the sunlight. At night, your parakeet will want ten hours of sleep. You may need to cover the cage with dark cloth. Now it's time to find your parakeet.

Picking Your Parakeet

The most important rule about picking a parakeet is also the hardest. *Take your time.* It's okay if you don't find one right away.

Pet stores have lots of choices. Find out where the bird came from. Make sure it is happy around people. In the U.S., parakeets sold at pet stores are American budgies. To buy the larger English budgie, you'll need to visit a **breeder**.

Breeders hand train their birds. They know about their bird's mom and dad. The breeder's place should be clean. Their birds should have plenty of room. Choose a parakeet that seems active and happy. It should have bright eyes and clean feathers.

Like people, parakeets often change when they are **adolescents**. Humans become teenagers at age 13. Parakeets behave like teens when they are a year old or so. They might start nipping, make more noise or seem mean. The good thing is this only lasts a few months. Sadly, this is when many parakeet owners give them up.

Adopting a parakeet means giving an unwanted pet a new home. It may take more time for it to bond with you. But there are many ways to help your parakeet be happy in its new home.

DID YOU KNOW?
If you are allergic to dogs or cats, you might be okay with a parakeet. That's because they don't shed much **dander.**

Parakeet Playtime

Playtime and training go together. Parakeets are **delicate**. They must be handled with care. Be gentle. Give them treats when they are good. *Never* yell or get angry when they don't do what you want or if they nip.

The best way to train your parakeet is to spend as much time as you can with it. Get close to your parakeet by teaching it to step up. At first, let it get used to its new home. Try sitting beside its cage and talking to it. Parakeets are great listeners!

After a few days, slowly approach the cage. Open the door. Put a treat in your hand and put it in the cage. Rest your hand on the bottom of the cage. If it comes over for the treat, praise it. After it gets used to this, move its perch. Push very gently on its belly. Say "up." If it jumps onto the perch, give it a treat. Later you can put your finger on its perch. Say "up." Soon it will know this trick.

If it backs away, give it space. If it hisses or puffs out its feathers, stop training for a while. Later, try giving it a treat through the bars. Always go slow.

The next step is letting it use your finger as a perch outside of its cage. Do this in a room where the windows and doors have been closed. It should be a room without a fireplace or any other pets. Always use the word "up" to get it to hop onto your finger.

Repeating the same word is also how you teach it to speak. It should be an easy word like hello. Say it face-to-face. It may take weeks or months, but your parakeet should learn to speak. After it can say one word, it will be much easier getting it to say more.

Parakeets have a low voice. Some are hard to understand. They can learn songs, too. Parakeet owners say boys are easier to train than girls. Even if it never learns to speak, show it you love it by spending lots of time with it and feeding it food it likes.

DID YOU KNOW?

Parakeets can be taught a large vocabulary. In fact, the Guinness Book of World Records has recognized a budgerigar as being "the most talking bird." Puck the Budgerigar has a vocabulary of over 1,700 words.

Eat Like a Bird

Have you heard someone say they eat like a bird? It's supposed to mean eating very little. The funny thing is for their size, birds eat a lot. Your parakeet will put away about four teaspoons of birdseed a day. That's one quarter of their weight. It's like a 100-pound person eating 25 pounds of food every day!

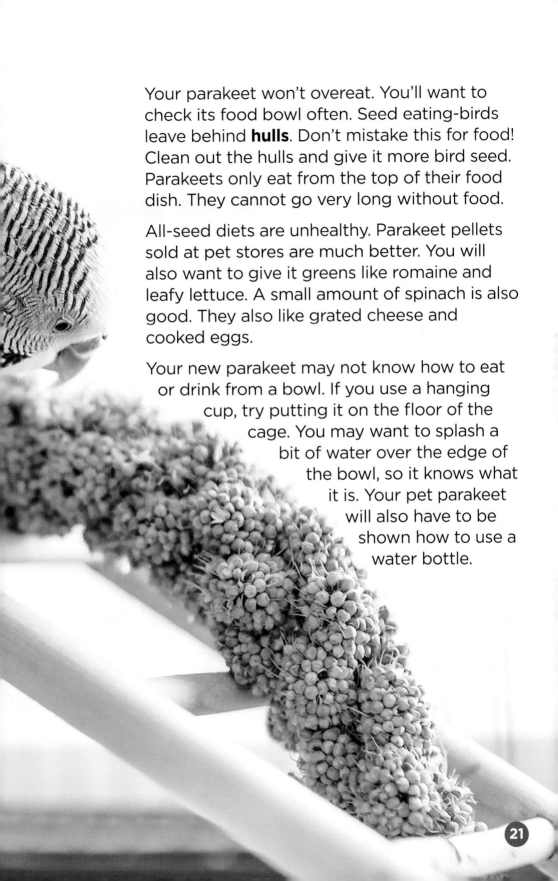

Your parakeet won't overeat. You'll want to check its food bowl often. Seed eating-birds leave behind **hulls**. Don't mistake this for food! Clean out the hulls and give it more bird seed. Parakeets only eat from the top of their food dish. They cannot go very long without food.

All-seed diets are unhealthy. Parakeet pellets sold at pet stores are much better. You will also want to give it greens like romaine and leafy lettuce. A small amount of spinach is also good. They also like grated cheese and cooked eggs.

Your new parakeet may not know how to eat or drink from a bowl. If you use a hanging cup, try putting it on the floor of the cage. You may want to splash a bit of water over the edge of the bowl, so it knows what it is. Your pet parakeet will also have to be shown how to use a water bottle.

Tap water often has **chlorine**. This is very dangerous for birds. Bottled, non-chlorinated water is best. Water and food should always be fresh. If there is any food left after a few hours throw it out. Parakeets are picky about the cleanliness of their water when they want to drink. It's also a good idea to clean the food dish completely every few days or whenever your bird makes a mess of the bowl.

Some food is dangerous. Parakeets can get sick if they eat food that has a lot of sugar. *Don't give your parakeet chocolate, avocados, guacamole, or anything with caffeine like soda, tea, or coffee.* Seeds from fruit are also bad.

Good food and water will help keep your parakeet healthy. Just like you, it will also need a checkup.

Keeping Your Parakeet Healthy

Parakeets have long lifespans. Your new bird might someday join you at college. The easiest way to keep your parakeet from getting sick is by spending time with it. You will know when it is acting differently. You will see right away if it stops eating or seems to have no energy.

Your parakeet should also visit a **veterinarian**. This is a doctor just for animals. Avian vets focus on birds. Bring your new budgie to a vet the first week it comes home. You should then take it for a checkup once a year.

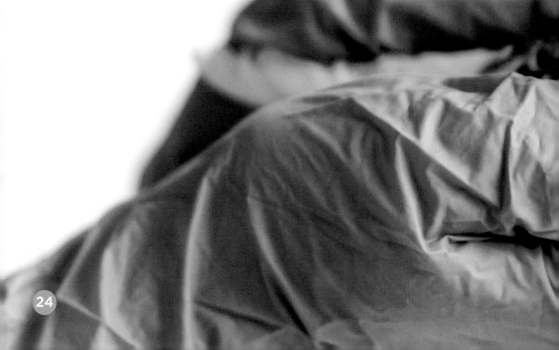

If your parakeet's beak swells or if it has been pulling out its feathers, it should go to the vet. If it sits on the floor of its cage and doesn't use a perch, it needs to see one as well.

Take good care of it. Dogs are often called people's best friends. But you might soon decide your parakeet is your best friend.

SHOPPING LIST

This is a list of some things your parakeet will need:

- ☐ Wire cage at least two feet long, wide and tall
- ☐ Cage cover
- ☐ Habitat paper or litter
- ☐ Budgie seed
- ☐ Parakeet pellets
- ☐ Water and food bowls
- ☐ Toys (ladders, ropes, bells, and balls)
- ☐ Birdbath
- ☐ Variety of perches
- ☐ Treats like millet spray, seed bars, and honey bells
- ☐ Bird safe disinfectant or vinegar

FIND OUT MORE

Online
There are several sites that will help you raise happy, healthy parakeets:

The Humane Society has information on parakeet care:
"Parakeet (budgerigar) Care." https://www.animalhumanesociety.org/adoption/parakeet-budgerigar-care

Petfinder connects people with adoptable animals. They have parakeets in their "bird" section:
https://www.petfinder.com/search/birds-for-adoption/?sort%5B0%5D=recently_added

The Phoenix Landing Organization can also help you find parakeets that need forever homes:
https://www.phoenixlanding.org/adoption.html

Books

Brannon, Cecelia H. *Pet Parakeets.* Berkeley Heights. N.J.:Enslow 2017.

Hughes, Catherine D., *Little kids first big book of birds*. Washington, D.C.: National Geographic Kids. 2016.

Jeffrey, Laura S. *Choosing a Bird: How to Choose and Care for a Bird*.

Berkeley Heights, N.J.:Enslow 2013.

GLOSSARY

adolescent
Time between childhood and adulthood

adoption
Taking care of someone without a family

bond
Strong connection

breeding
Mating animals to produce similar ones

breeders
People who keep or take care of animals in order to produce similar ones

companion
Friend or buddy

chlorine
Dangerous greenish gas that is safe in very small amounts

dander
Loose scales shed from the skin that is carried on an animal's feathers or fur

delicate
Fragile, easily harmed

fumes
Gas or smoke with a strong smell that can be dangerous

habits
Regular behavior

hulls
Outer covering of a seed

mimic
Imitate, trying to sound like someone else

perch
Branches, posts or poles

popular
Well-liked

social
Happiest in a group

texture
The feel of a surface

veterinarian
Doctor who specializes in animal care

BIBLIOGRAPHY

"Are You Ready for a Pet Bird?" *VetBabble*. March 5, 2019. https://www.vetbabble.com/birds/are-you-ready/

"Bird Training Guide for Beginners." *VetBabble*. February 15, 2019. https://www.vetbabble.com/birds/bird-tricks-bird-training-guide-beginners/

Darling, Leslie. "Five Most Common House Pets." *The Nest*. https://pets.thenest.com/5-common-house-pets-4759.html

Hess, DVM, Diplomate ABVP (Avian Practice), Laurie. "The Four Most Important Things Your Bird Needs to Know." *Petmd*. https://www.petmd.com/bird/training/four-most-important-things-your-bird-needs-know

"How to Train Birds Not to Bite." *Petmd*. https://www.petmd.com/bird/training/how-train-birds-not-bite

"How to Care for Your Budgie (Parakeet)." Puppies are Prozac. http://puppiesareprozac.com/budgie-parakeet/care-articles-links/

"How to Teach an Old Bird New 'Tricks.'" *Petmd*. https://www.petmd.com/bird/training/evr_bd_oldbirds_newtricks

"Hypoallergenic Bird Species." Petmd. https://www.petmd.com/bird/wellness/evr_bd_hypoallergenic_bird_species

Kalhagen, Alyson. "Birds That Make Great Pets for Kids." *The Spruce Pets*. July 7, 2018. https://www.thesprucepets.com/three-birds-great-pets-for-kids-390539

"Choosing a Bird Cage: Rules to Remember." *The Spruce Pets*. January 13, 2019. https://www.thesprucepets.com/rules-on-choosing-a-bird-cage-390333

"Five Friendly Bird Species That Make Fantastic Pets." *The Spruce Pets*. September 9, 2018. https://www.thesprucepets.com/top-friendly-pet-bird-species-390535

"Lineolated Parakeet (Barred Parakeet): A Quiet, Easy-to-Manage Small Parrot." *The Spruce Pets*. July 22, 2018. https://www.thesprucepets.com/lineolated-parakeets-as-pets-390919

Kruzer, RVT. Adrienne. "Bird Cage Sizes and Bar Spacing." *The Spruce Pets*. February 03, 2019. https://www.thesprucepets.com/bird-cage-sizes-4065662, https://www.thesprucepets.com/bird-cage-sizes-4065662

LaBue, Vanessa Voltolina. How to Shoulder Train Your Bird." *Petmd*. https://www.petmd.com/bird/training/how-shoulder-train-your-bird

McLeod, DVM. Lianne. "Before You Choose A Pet Bird." *The Spruce Pets*. March 15, 2018. https://www.thesprucepets.com/before-you-choose-a-pet-bird-1238431

"Budgie (Parakeet)." *The Spruce Pets*. May 5, 2019. https://www.thesprucepets.com/budgies-1236736

"Parakeet (budgerigar) Care." The Animal Humane Society. https://www.animalhumanesociety.org/adoption/parakeet-budgerigar-care

Schnell, Lindsay. "Silver Medalist Morris Pitches Her Sport." *USA Today*. June 19, 2018, p. 04C.

Sund, Patricia. "Ten Super Vegetables for Your Parrots." *The Spruce Pets*. March 25, 2019. https://www.thesprucepets.com/super-vegetables-for-your-parrots-390197

"When is a Cage Not a Cage? When it's a Home." *The Spruce Pet*s. April 4, 2017. https://www.thesprucepets.com/the-term-cage-is-outdated-390350

"Top Three 'Starter' Birds." *Petmd*. https://www.petmd.com/bird/pet_lover/evr_bd_starter_birds

"Top 10 'Talking' Birds." *Petmd*. https://www.petmd.com/bird/top_tens/evr_bd_top10talking_birds

INDEX

ABOUT THE AUTHOR

John Bankston

The author of over 100 books for young readers, John Bankston lives in Miami Beach, Florida with his rescue dog Astronaut. He never realized how smart and friendly parakeets were until he wrote this book—which is one reason he loved writing it.